FEMINIST
CROSS-STITCH

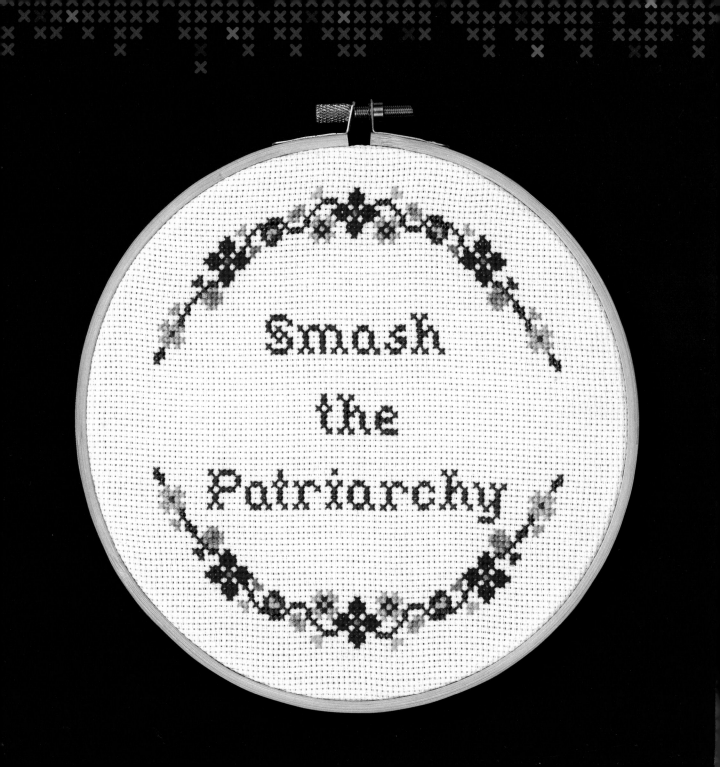

FEMINIST
CROSS-STITCH

40 Bold & Fierce Patterns

STEPHANIE ROHR

LARK
New York

LARK

New York

An Imprint of Sterling Publishing Co., Inc.
1166 Avenue of the Americas
New York, NY 10036

ISBN 978-1-4547-1080-6

Distributed in Canada by Sterling Publishing Co., Inc.
c/o Canadian Manda Group, 664 Annette Street
Toronto, Ontario M6S 2C8, Canada
Distributed in the United Kingdom by GMC Distribution Services
Castle Place, 166 High Street, Lewes, East Sussex BN7 1XU, England
Distributed in Australia by NewSouth Books
University of New South Wales, Sydney, NSW 2052, Australia

For information about custom editions, special sales, and premium and corporate purchases,
please contact Sterling Special Sales at 800-805-5489 or specialsales@sterlingpublishing.com.

Manufactured in China

2 4 6 8 10 9 7 5 3 1

larkcrafts.com
sterlingpublishing.com

Interior design by Shannon Nicole Plunkett
Cover design by Elizabeth Mihaltse Lindy
Photography by Christopher Bain

For my mother, Ann Rohr,
who taught me to cross-stitch, among (many) other things

For my Grandma Dee Troske,
who inspires me to always work hard and be kind

For my Nana Rohr,
who showed me how to speak my mind: firmly and with wit

CONTENTS

INTRODUCTION

I have been surrounded by cross-stitch for most of my life. My siblings and I grew up with baby samplers in each of our bedrooms, and as a child I would watch my mother work on beautiful landscape scenes, quilt blocks, and traditional cross-stitch projects like birth announcements and alphabet samplers. (It was the '80s—there were lots of pastels.) When I was five, she bought me a kid-friendly cross-stitch kit with a simple little butterfly design. I was instantly hooked! I continued cross-stitching as a relaxing hobby throughout my early teens. I lost interest because there weren't any designs that appealed to me anymore, but I couldn't stay away from stitching for long. I picked it up again in my early twenties and soon decided that my desire to stitch exactly what I wanted meant that I should start designing patterns myself.

When I began my cross-stitching career in 2010, my designs were more in line with the subversive cross-stitch movement that began in the early 2000s.

I was pairing delicate flowers and cutesy geometrics with curse words, pop culture references, and humorous phrases. The designs were fun and intricate, but the messages were more escapist than activist.

Then the 2016 US presidential election happened. My creations suddenly took a turn. I began seeking out phrases with a political and specifically feminist focus. I wanted to feel empowered and inspire other people to feel the same way. The designs ranged from hopeful phrases of gentle encouragement to full-on NSFW rage directed at the patriarchy. They took off. When I looked at my online sales, feedback on social media, and interactions with customers at in-person events, I saw that I wasn't the only one who needed these messages and the therapeutic benefits of cross-stitch. Although the election sparked my need to create feminist designs, these patterns go far beyond this moment in time. As I continue to focus on feminist designs, they have become less of a reaction to current events and more of a central tenet of my art. Striving for equality will be an ongoing battle, and the desire to lift up and support one another is timeless. Cross-stitch is the perfect medium for these messages.

In the past, cross-stitch was viewed as "women's work." Learning to sew, knit, and embroider were part of a girl's education in many parts of the world. Many young women used cross-stitch samplers to practice alphabets and simple motifs that they would later stitch onto clothing and household items. Needlework crafts were not only practical; they were also used as a form of protest or an expression of patriotism. Working in groups also allowed women to get together and discuss important topics, debate, and plan for change. During the American Revolution, women spun their own wool to avoid using boycotted British textiles for soldiers' uniforms. Antislavery sewing circles were common in the antebellum era in the US. This craftivist tradition continues into the present day, whether in the form of the AIDS Memorial Quilt, started in 1985, or the pink Pussyhats™ made and worn by participants in the 2016 Women's Marches.

I am thrilled to cross-stitch at a time when this traditional art form is not only being recognized as art for its own sake but when it also allows people to express their opinions, show support for marginalized groups, and protest. No longer seen as just women's work, cross-stitch is a creative outlet available to anyone who is interested in picking up a needle and thread.

As you learn to stitch and work through the patterns in this book, I encourage you to cross-stitch in any way you want. You can work on a project slowly over weeks or even months, picking it up when you have a chance. You can also burn through a project all in one sitting. It can be a great way to make affordable gifts for friends and family or to decorate your home or workspace. You can invite friends over for social stitching sessions. You may be inspired to start designing your own patterns or even start your own business. There is no limit to the ways you can make a statement using cross-stitch!

CROSS-STITCH BASICS

Cross-stitch is for everyone (just like feminism!). It is one of the easiest needlecrafts for a total beginner to pick up. Can you sew *X*s on a grid? Then you can cross-stitch! Even if sewing isn't your thing, don't worry. (Confession: I can't sew, knit, or do any other cool needlework! It's cross-stitch or nothing for me.) This how-to section will tell you everything you need to know, even if you've never touched a needle and thread in your life.

Cross-stitch is a type of *embroidery*, which is an umbrella term for all crafts that involve decorating fabric with thread. While other types of embroidery let you "paint" or "draw" with thread to make freeform images, cross-stitch involves counting and working on a grid, and it must always be done by hand. In this way, it resembles mosaic art, pointillism, or modern pixel art more than drawing or painting.

SUPPLIES

To begin any cross-stitch project, you only need a few supplies. Supplies for cross-stitch can be found at any craft and fabric store, as well as at many online retailers. There are also several specialized sites that sell cross-stitch supplies. (For a list of places to start, flip to Resources on page 119.)

AIDA CLOTH

Aida cloth is made specifically for cross-stitch and embroidery. It is a cotton even-weave fabric, meaning it is woven with small holes placed at even intervals. This creates a grid of squares that will correspond exactly to the grid on a cross-stitch pattern. Adia cloth comes in many different fabric counts, which describe the number of squares per inch in the fabric. The projects in this book use 14-count and 16-count Aida cloth.

You can find Aida in precut sizes, the smallest (and most common) being 15 × 18 inches (38.1 × 45.7 cm). Each pattern in this book will suggest a size and color for the Aida, but you can feel free to experiment! In general, a higher count number will make the stitches, as well as the final project size, smaller and the stitching more challenging. The opposite is true for smaller count sizes. Black or dark-colored Aida can look great, but if you're a new stitcher, it might be tougher to work with because the holes are harder to see.

It is also possible to stitch on other fabrics, such as even-weave linen. However, I recommend Aida for beginner stitchers because the visible "grid" on linen is much smaller and a bit more difficult to navigate. Aida makes it much easier to keep the sizes of your stitches uniform.

EMBROIDERY FLOSS

You'll use embroidery floss to stitch your project. Embroidery floss consists of six small strands that are twisted together. It is often made of cotton. For the projects in this book, you will use either two or three strands at a time, depending on the fabric count of your Aida. For pieces using 14-count Aida, you will use three strands. For pieces using 16-count Aida, you will use two strands.

Embroidery floss comes in hundreds of colors, each with its own number. The numbering system depends on the manufacturer of the floss. This book lists the numbers for floss from DMC®, one of the most common brands in the US. If you are using a different brand, there are conversion charts available online to help you match the colors, or you can eyeball them yourself. Each pattern will list the colors you'll need for the project, or you can create your own custom color palettes.

NEEDLE

The best needles for cross-stitching are tapestry needles. They have blunt ends and large eyes. You don't need a sharp needle since the Aida cloth already has holes, and the large eye of the tapestry needle makes it easier to thread. The needle size you use will depend on the Aida count. Just like with Aida cloth, the higher the needle size, the smaller the needle. Use a size 24 tapestry needle for 14-count Aida and a size 26 needle for 16-count Aida.

EMBROIDERY HOOP

An embroidery hoop holds your fabric taut and makes it easier to stitch. It consists of two

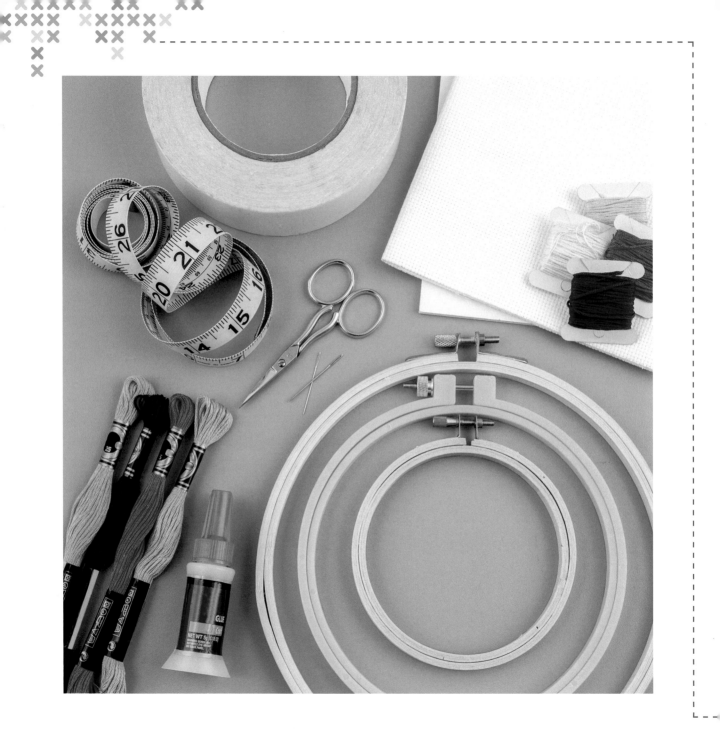

concentric rings made of wood, bamboo, or plastic. The outer ring has a small opening and a screw that you can tighten or loosen. Hoops are measured by their diameter and range from 3 inches (7.6 cm) to 10 inches (25.4 cm) wide. Plastic hoops tend to be sturdier than wood or bamboo hoops and can be used over and over again for different projects. Smaller hoops made from plastic also tend to hold the tension on your fabric better. Instead of using a larger 10-inch (25.4 cm) hoop for an 8 × 10–inch (20.3 × 25.4 cm) piece, try a 6-inch (15.2 cm) or 7-inch (17.8 cm) hoop and move it around to different areas of the fabric as you stitch. For circular pieces, you may even want to stitch in a plastic hoop and then frame in a wooden one later.

Hoops are a great tool for framing and displaying your finished piece. For a circular piece, use a wood or bamboo hoop of the size specified for both stitching and framing. If you plan to display your piece in a traditional picture frame instead, you can use a plastic hoop of any size. To place your fabric in a hoop, first loosen the outer ring and separate it from the inner ring. Lay the inner ring on a flat surface, place the fabric on top of it, and then put the outer hoop over both the fabric and the inner hoop. Press down and then tighten the screw so that the fabric is stretched tightly, like a drum.

SCISSORS

When it comes to cutting fabric or trimming a piece of thread, any pair of scissors will do. If you want to be fancy, you can use embroidery scissors. These are small and super-sharp. Their pointy ends help you snip the end of a thread without snagging the stitches near it. You can also use them to snip individual stitches and fix any mistakes you may make.

MEASURING TOOL

You will need measuring tape or a ruler to make sure your fabric is the right size for the project.

BOBBINS (OPTIONAL)

Bobbins are used for storing your embroidery floss and keeping your floss collection neat and organized. They resemble flat spools and are made of cardboard or plastic. You can wind your floss around them and write the floss number at the space on the top or bottom. Bobbins are optional but especially fun if you love to organize your craft stash.

FRAMING SUPPLIES

Once your project is finished, you will want to display it proudly for all to see. I will cover how to frame in a later section (page 23), but here is what you will need.

If you're framing your piece in a hoop, you'll need a wooden hoop, scissors, and paint-on craft glue. Optional supplies include felt or fabric to cover the back of the hoop.

If you're using a traditional frame, you'll need a photo frame, mat board, and stitchery tape, which is a type of double-sided tape with an adhesive that won't damage or discolor fabric or thread. It is best to choose a deep photo frame—one that has enough space between the glass and removable back to hold the Aida cloth. In some cases, you will have room to insert a mat board. In other cases, the space is tight enough to hold the piece up against the glass.

PREPARING TO STITCH

Now that you have your materials, I'm sure you're ready to get started! But before you dive into the stitching, there are a few more things you'll need to do.

FIND YOUR STITCHING SPOT

Good lighting is very important for cross-stitch. Looking at detailed patterns and focusing on your stitching can cause eyestrain and even migraines. (And stitching is supposed to be fun!) It is best to sit near a window with natural sunlight or directly under a lamp or other light source. I have a clip-on LED light with a bendy neck that I can point over my shoulder. I have even seen people use more creative lighting solutions, like headlamps, music stand lights, or reading lights. If you are stitching on dark-colored Aida, it will help to have an additional light source underneath your hoop. The holes are harder to see on dark cloth, and the backlighting will really help them stand out.

In addition to proper lighting, your stitching spot should include a comfy seat. You can stitch on the couch, in a chair, or at a table. It is also a good idea to wash your hands before handling the Aida cloth, as it will attract dirt and the natural oils on your hands.

Most importantly, your stitching spot should be a happy one. This is your chance to relax and create.

CHOOSE YOUR PATTERN

The patterns in this book are marked using icons with four different skill levels: Newbie, Beginner, Intermediate, and Advanced. These levels are based on a few general guidelines. Newbie patterns are smaller and more symmetrical, use fewer floss colors, and are stitched on 14-count Aida.

Intermediate patterns are generally larger, include more floss colors, and use Aida with a higher stitch count. Intermediate patterns may not be symmetrical and can include backstitches (page 20) and fractional stitches (page 20). Beginner patterns fall somewhere between Newbie and Intermediate.

If you have never stitched before, I would recommend jumping in with a Newbie pattern. If you have one or two projects under your belt, you can choose a Beginner pattern. For more experienced stitchers, go nuts with an Intermediate pattern! Finally, if you are really up for a challenge or want a more long-term project, you can tackle the Advanced "Rosie the Riveter" pattern. But at the end of the day, the most important thing is to choose a project that speaks to you, amuses you, and inspires you to create.

LEVEL ICONS

NEWBIE

BEGINNER

INTERMEDIATE

ADVANCED

READING THE PATTERN

A cross-stitch pattern looks a lot like the image of the finished piece, but instead of stitches, there are colored squares with symbols. Each symbol represents a specific thread color, and every pattern has a key that tells you which threads correspond to which symbols. The squares are laid out on a grid that matches the grid of the Aida cloth. The pattern grid is numbered on the sides to help you count the squares and to show the total size of the design. Each square with a symbol is one full cross-stitch. Fractional stitches will appear as half-filled squares, and backstitches will be marked with lines. The corners of each square represent the holes in the Aida cloth.

CROSS-STITCH

FRACTIONAL STITCH

BACKSTITCH

GET YOUR AIDA READY

Always stitch on a piece of Aida that is larger than the finished piece. You'll want to leave at least an extra inch (2.5 cm) all around for pieces that will be displayed in photo frames and an extra 2 inches (5.1 cm) for pieces framed in hoops. It is best to leave more fabric around a circular design, since some of the cloth is lost when you hold the Aida in a hoop. For example, if you're placing a finished piece in a 5 × 7–inch (12.7 × 17.8 cm) frame, your fabric should be at least 6 × 8–inch (15.2 × 20.3 cm). If you're using a 6-inch (15.2 cm) hoop, it should be at least 8 × 8–inch (20.3 × 20.3 cm). For frames, you can use your measuring tape or ruler and scissors to cut your Aida to the proper size. If you're planning to display your piece in a hoop, you can simply place the large piece of fabric into the hoop and then cut around the ring. Remember, in either case, you can always trim away extra Aida, but you can't add more if you run out of space to stitch!

Before placing your fabric in your hoop find the center of your Aida cloth. Fold your fabric in half twice, once crosswise and once lengthwise. Then unfold the cloth and center your hoop over the point where the creases intersect. Make sure the hoop is screwed on tightly and pull the fabric tight within the hoop. If you want to be exact about the center, you can count the number of squares from the top of the hoop, right below the screw closure, to the bottom of the hoop. Divide that number in two and recount from the top of the closure until you reach the halved number. But if you have enough extra fabric, approximating the center will be fine.

PREPARE YOUR EMBROIDERY FLOSS

To divide your floss, first cut a 12- to 18-inch (30.5 cm to 45.7 cm) length from your skein. (Use your measuring tape if you're not comfortable eyeballing it!) Hold it up, grab the desired number of strands, and gently pull the strands apart. I like to wind my remaining strands around the skein of floss so it doesn't sit in a tangled clump. Keeping the strands with the floss (or bobbins) also prevents mix-ups when you're working with similar colors.

THREAD YOUR NEEDLE

Threading a needle for cross-stitch is fairly easy, even if you've been traumatized by previous needle-threading experiences. Tapestry needles have very large eyes, making threading much easier. Hold your strands of thread close to the ends. Make sure the ends are lined up perfectly, and poke them through the eye of the needle. Once they begin coming through the eye, grab the ends from the opposite side of the needle and pull them through further, leaving a tail about 2 inches (5.1 cm) long.

If this is proving difficult, you can wet the end of the thread, either in your mouth or with a bit of water. (Don't worry, folks—any "moistened" bit of thread will be cut off eventually and won't be in the final product.) Once it's a little wet, flatten the thread between your finger and thumb. The eye of the needle is more oval than circular, so you can turn your flattened thread accordingly and push it through.

LOCATE YOUR STARTING POINT

When starting a new pattern, it is best to begin at the center, which is located at the intersection of the red lines on the patterns. On the sides of the pattern, there are also arrows marking the center of each axis. Sometimes the first stitch is exactly at the center of the pattern. If it's not, simply count over, up, or down from the center to find your first stitch.

ESSENTIAL STITCHES AND TECHNIQUES

When it comes right down to it, cross-stitching is about manipulating thread into an image. This section will get into the nitty-gritty of how you will bend the thread to your creative will.

KNOTTING YOUR THREAD

Knots (or the absence of knots) have always been a contentious topic for cross-stitchers. It all depends on how much you care about the back of your piece. Knots don't look as good, but because they're in the back, theoretically no one else will see them. Plus, knots will help prevent you from pulling the entire thread through your piece and can be a good way to start for a newbie who just wants to start stitching as soon as possible.

KNOT

If you just want to get started and don't mind a messy back, simply tie a small knot in the end of your thread that is too large to pull through your Aida. This usually means knotting the thread at the same spot twice. Some old-school or purist stitchers will say this is a no-no and insist that the back of your piece should look as beautiful as the front. I personally am in the "stitch however the hell you want" camp. Just be aware that if you are going to frame your piece in a traditional frame, knots can make the surface a bit lumpy. Knots are better for more forgiving hoop frames.

After you've knotted your thread, start your first stitch by drawing your needle and thread from the back side of the fabric to the front and then stitch away like the rebel you are.

WASTE KNOT

Want the ease of a knot and a neat back? Waste knots are for you! This method works if you're stitching with either two or three strands.

1. Tie a knot (or two) near the end of your thread.

2. Bring the thread through the fabric from the back side to make your first stitch. Don't pull the knot all the way up against the fabric; leave an inch or two (2.5 or 5.1 cm) of thread between the knot and the back. Hold this extra thread down and stitch over it as you make your first cross-stitches (**A**).

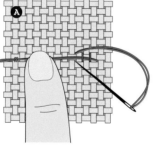

BACK SIDE OF FABRIC

3. Once the thread is secured with at least four stitches on the back side, cut off the extra floss. It's like it was never there!

LOOP METHOD

This knotless technique is for the super-neat folks out there and works when you're using two strands to stitch. You will have the flattest back in all the land with the loop method.

1. Cut your floss double the length that you plan to use and separate out just one strand.

2. Fold the strand in half so that you have two ends on one side and a loop on the other side.

3. Thread the needle using the side that has both ends of the floss.

4. Take the threaded needle and come through the back of the fabric to start a regular cross-stitch. Stitch the first half of the *X* and move your needle to the back again, making sure to leave some extra slack on the loop at the back of the fabric (**B**).

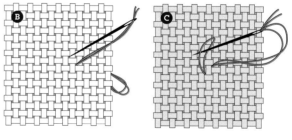

BACK SIDE OF FABRIC

5. Flip your fabric over so you can see the back and guide your needle through the loop of floss (**C**). Gently pull tight so that the loop flattens against the back.

6. With your needle, come through the back again to finish the second diagonal of the cross-stitch and then just keep stitching!

THE CROSS-STITCH

Here it is: the basic cross-stitch. An *X*. Don't be fooled by its simple appearance, however. This little stitch is the building block for your sassy phrases, your fabulous florals, and your gorgeous geometrics! I like to think of the cross-stitch as the invention of the pixel hundreds of years before its time. Using this versatile stitch, you can make something as simple as a straight line or something as complex as a photorealistic human face.

1. Start by drawing your needle from the back of the fabric to the front side, through the lower-left corner of the square you are starting on (**D**). Gently pull the thread all the way through.

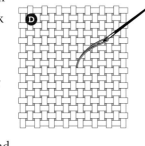

2. Insert the needle through the hole diagonally to the right (**E**). Again, pull the

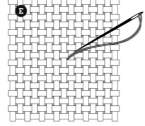

thread through toward the back. You have now made a half stitch (see "Fractional Stitches," page 20)!

3. Now draw the needle to the front again, this time through the lower-right corner of the square (**F**).

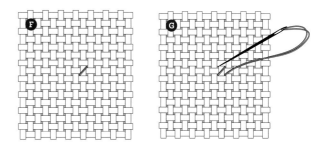

4. Finish the *X* by putting the needle through the upper-left corner (**G**). Pull the needle all the way through to the back, and you have made a cross-stitch! Look at you go!

It doesn't matter which diagonal ends up on the top of the cross-stitch. However, you do want it to remain uniform throughout the piece. I tend to stitch the bottom of my stitches using a right-leaning diagonal and my tops with a left-leaning one, but there is no right or wrong way to do it.

Some people prefer to make one full cross-stitch at a time as they work through their pattern. If you want to make the next stitch in the row using this approach, the next step would be to come through the lower-left corner of the adjacent square and start the process over again (**H**).

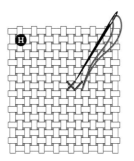

You can also make a row of by first creating a line of half stitches, then coming back and stitching the opposite diagonal, which completes the *X*. This is particularly helpful when you're working on a long row or a large area that uses the same color. First, stitch along the row and make the diagonals between the lower-left to upper-right corner of each square (**I**). Then stitch along the same row in the opposite direction with diagonals between the lower-right to upper-left corners (**J**).

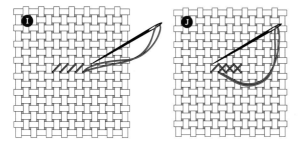

FRACTIONAL STITCHES

In addition to the full cross-stitch, there are also fractional stitches, which are named because they only take up a fraction of the square. We have already covered the half stitch in steps 1, 2, and 4

of the cross-stitch instructions—it is simply one diagonal of the *X*. The only other fractional stitch used in this book is the three-quarter stitch.

To make a three-quarter stitch, you make the first short diagonal by poking the needle through the fabric at the center of the square (**K**), then finishing the second diagonal like a normal cross-stitch (**L**).

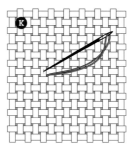
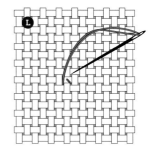

BACKSTITCH

The backstitch can be used to outline and add detail to cross-stitched images, and it can also be used to create letters.

1. To make a horizontal backstitch, start from the back of the fabric and bring your needle to the front through the lower-left corner. Bring it to the back again through the lower-right corner (**M**).

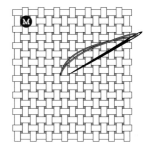

2. From the back side of the fabric, bring your needle to the front through the lower-left corner of the next square.

3. Move your needle back (Get it? Backstitch?) toward your previous stitch, pushing your needle through the same corner that you used to start your backstitch (**N**).

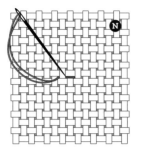

4. Sometimes, the backstitch will go diagonally over two squares. Just continue with the same method that you used to make a straight line (**O**).

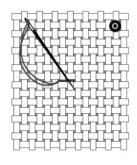

When stitching a letter using backstitch, you might change direction many times and switch between straight and diagonal lines. Just keep following these same steps as you stitch.

CARRYING A THREAD

In many of the patterns in this book, each color will appear in many different areas of the design. There are a couple of ways to handle this. One way is to finish the thread (which will be explained in the next section) and then start stitching again in the next area. Another way is to carry the thread over the back side of the fabric to the next spot it's needed (**P**). It is best to carry thread over a small distance, where there are no gaps in the stitching. If needed, I would recommend only carrying over five to six blank squares. This is especially important if you are using a dark-colored floss, as it could possibly show through to the front. However, you can carry a thread over a larger distance and avoid this problem if there are already stitches through which you can weave the thread.

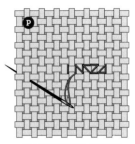

BACK SIDE OF FABRIC

FINISHING A THREAD

When you are finished with a color, whether because there are no more stitches to make in a specific area, or because your thread is getting too short to work with, simply tuck your needle under at least three previously sewn stitches on the back side of your piece and pull the thread through (**Q**). Trim any extra thread.

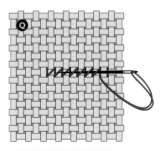

BACK SIDE OF FABRIC

CROSS-STITCH TROUBLESHOOTING

PROBLEM: My thread keeps twisting and/or tying itself in knots!

SOLUTION: It is common for the working thread to twist, which can lead to spontaneous knots. This is annoying but easy to fix. If you notice your thread starting to wind over itself, simply let go of your needle, hold your hoop up, and let the needle dangle. The thread will untwist itself!

PROBLEM: I miscounted my stitches and spaces!

SOLUTION: One of the many beauties of cross-stitch is that nothing is permanent or unfixable. Unthread your needle and locate the first miscounted stitch. Then use your needle to start un-stitching your work. (When you have a lot of stitches to pull out, this process is known as *frogging*, because you have to "rip it, rip it!") I like to use my needle to slide under the last stitch and then pull it up to loosen it. Keep pulling until the end of the thread is pulled through. Continue working backward until you reach the miscounted stitch. It's the cross-stitch version of rewinding.

If your mistake doesn't really bother you, it's totally okay to just . . . not fix it. Cross-stitching is supposed to be fun. If having an asymmetrical finished project would decidedly not be fun for you, then by all means frog it and fix it. If you'd rather just keep stitching, then just continue with the pattern. I promise not to tell.

PROBLEM: I stitched the floss tail into the design!

SOLUTION: Don't panic. It's perfectly normal to get into the flow of stitching and lose track of the tail at the end of your thread. You will know this has happened when your stitches are suddenly twice as chunky and instead of a loose end of thread in your needle, you have a loop that is connected to the cloth. In this case, don't cut the floss. (You won't know which end is the "main" thread and which end is the "tail.") Instead, rewind. Turn your needle around and start undoing your stitches. After each stitch you undo, gently tug on the needle and see if the end frees itself. Repeat this process until the end emerges. Once the issue is resolved, check in periodically and make sure your floss tail remains about one third the length of the rest of your thread.

PROBLEM: I keep losing my place in the pattern!

SOLUTION: Make a "working copy" of your pattern by photocopying the page, then use a highlighter to mark the stitches you have completed. Another option is to place a small sticky note on the page to mark where you left off.

FINISHING AND FRAMING YOUR PIECE

Once you are done stitching, you can frame your piece either in your embroidery hoop or in a more traditional picture frame. But before you frame, there are a few optional steps you can take to make sure your piece looks its best.

WASHING YOUR PIECE

It is normal for the fabric to get a bit dirty while stitching, even just from the natural oils on your hands. To wash your piece, first run it under cold water, then gently hand-wash it in a clean sink, using a small amount of dish soap or mild detergent. Rinse all the soap out with cold water. Do not wring it dry. Instead, roll it between two towels and then leave it flat to air-dry.

IRONING YOUR PIECE

You will usually only need to iron your piece if you used a hoop to stitch it but are planning to hang it in a picture frame. Ironing will get "hoop marks" and any other creases and wrinkles out. To iron, turn the piece over, stitched pattern facing down, and iron the back on a low setting. To avoid flattening your stitches, do not press hard. For extra protection against flattened stitches, you can put a towel or other fabric barrier between the iron and your piece. If there is a stubborn hoop mark on an area with no stitches, you can turn the iron up to a higher setting to remove it.

DISPLAYING IN AN EMBROIDERY HOOP

There are many ways to finish a cross-stitch in a wooden hoop, but I am going to describe one of the simplest methods, which is also the method I like.

1. Make sure that your piece is completely centered in the hoop and that the Aida fabric is pulled tight. Tighten the screw closure as much as you can, and make sure that it is centered at the top of the hoop. This is important, because you will use the screw closure to hang the piece.

2. Once your piece is centered, trim away any extra fabric around the edges of the hoop, leaving just enough to fold over the inner edge of the hoop.

3. Brush a thin layer of all-purpose glue inside the inner hoop to affix the cut edges. Make sure the edges don't overlap onto the back of the actual piece, as this will show through. Press the glued fabric down.

4. If you want to cover the back of the hoop, first layer the back of your piece with felt or another fabric that is the same size as your Aida cloth. Put the hoop over both the felt and the cross-stitched fabric and repeat the steps outlined above. You can also cut out a circle of felt and glue that separately to the back of the hoop, on the outer rim.

DISPLAYING IN A PHOTO FRAME

I have designed all of my pieces to fit in standard-size photo frames. Simply trim the Aida fabric down to the size of the frame, insert your piece into the space where the photo would normally go, and then put the back of the frame over it. The frame should hold your piece tightly against the glass.

If you are concerned about wrinkles or how much space is around the edges of your frame, you can place a mat board behind your piece.

1. Trim your piece to the size of the frame, making sure there is a small amount of fabric that can fold over the back of the mat at each straight edge.

2. Use stitchery tape to attach your piece to the mat. Unroll the tape and cut it into pieces that will cover the front of the mat. Put the sticky side of the tape down on to the mat.

3. When the piece is centered and stretched over the mat to your liking, peel off the paper on the second side of the tape and press your piece onto it. Then fold the extra fabric over the back, once again securing it with tape.

4. Insert the whole thing into the frame, and you're done!

PROFESSIONAL FRAMING

If you have expended all of your crafty energy on stitching your project, feel free to take your piece to a professional framer. Or ask a professional just because you want to be fancy.

A FINAL NOTE:
STITCH THE WAY YOU WANT

All of these instructions reflect the way I, personally, stitch—the way my mother taught me to. One of the beautiful things about this craft is the fact that it has been passed down through the generations. There are many variations in these methods, and you may find a different way to cross-stitch that works better for you. Maybe you like to start in the corner of a design. Maybe you like to stitch one color at a time or one section at a time. Maybe you like using four strands to stitch with, or just one! Feel free to experiment with the fabric and colors you use, and adapt the stitches and techniques based on how you want to display your finished work. Are you good at sewing? Turn your piece into a pillow, or incorporate it onto a patch that you sew onto an item of clothing. Make it into a bookmark, a magnet, or an ornament. The possibilities are endless, and there really is no "wrong" way to cross-stitch. It should be a fun, relaxing way to express your creativity. You get to decide what that means.

STITCHED AFFIRMATIONS

This collection of designs, featuring some of the first feminist patterns
I designed, is made to invigorate and inspire. They are about celebrating
yourself, standing up for yourself, and taking care of yourself.
They cover themes ranging from body positivity and supporting others
to letting your voice be heard. If you're looking for a project with
encouraging words, this is the place to find it.

FITS A 4 × 6-INCH (10.2 × 15.2 CM) FRAME WHEN STITCHED ON 14-COUNT AIDA

SAFE SPACE

This design is a beautiful way to let people know that they are in a space where they can feel empowered to truly be themselves, free of not just sexism but other discriminatory isms or phobias.

Symbol	Color
3	3855
■	310
◖	3838
◆	3801
◣	992
▼	977
⬇	208

POWER

"Girl power" is a phrase that everyone has heard, but I prefer this graphic depiction of female strength, with the iconic Venus symbol incorporated into the word *power*. With its simple border and two-tone design, this would be a great first project.

▲ ▶ 310

◄ ▶ 915

LET THEM HEAR YOU ROAR

This sweet little stitch encourages you to speak out and find your voice. Actually, don't just speak out—roar and make sure your voice is heard. Navy-blue fabric makes the colors pop, but this piece would work with a lighter color as well.

⬤ ▬ 3776

✳ ▬ 168

◆ ▬ 563

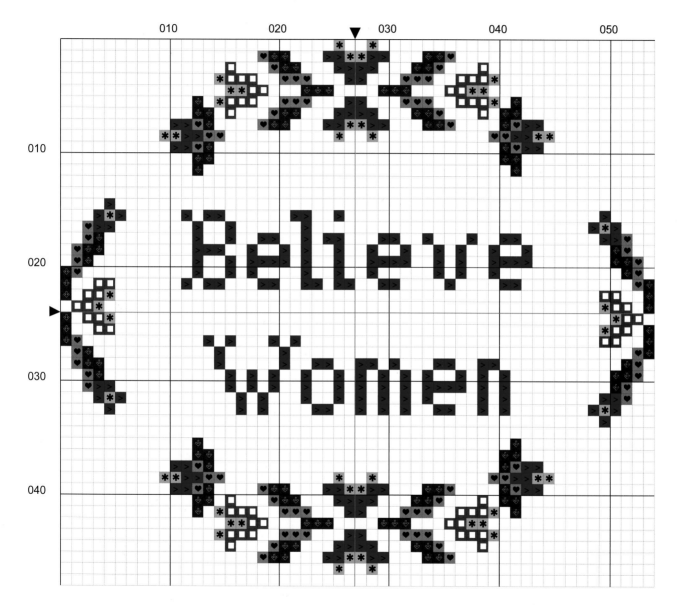

BELIEVE WOMEN

These words are simple to say and simple to stitch, but unfortunately have not always been simple to do. In 2017 the United States saw the rise of the #MeToo movement, with thousands of people bravely coming forward to share their experiences of sexual harassment and sexual assault. These stories brought attention to the institutional and individual biases that still make it hard for survivors of sexual harassment or sexual assault to be heard. This piece uses bold red text and soft folk-art-inspired borders to get the message across.

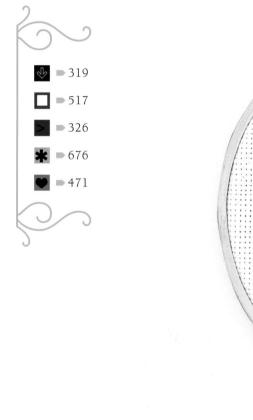

⬇ ➡ 319

▢ ➡ 517

▷ ➡ 326

✳ ➡ 676

♥ ➡ 471

SMASH THE PATRIARCHY

Everyone could use a daily reminder to fight the patriarchy, especially in floral cross-stitched form. Although this piece fits a larger hoop, it is very beginner-friendly, as the stitch count is low.

- ➨ 3354
- ➨ 915
- ➨ 561
- ➨ 3837
- ➨ 721
- ➨ 3755
- ➨ 972

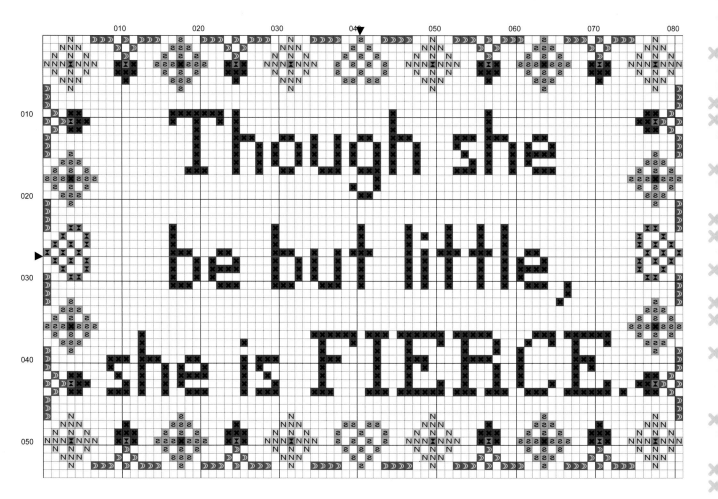

THOUGH SHE BE BUT LITTLE, SHE IS FIERCE

I am a theater nerd at heart, so I had to include a Shakespeare quote in this collection. This one comes from *A Midsummer Night's Dream* and describes Helena, who is physically small but strong and feisty. Shakespeare wrote during a time when women weren't allowed onstage, yet he penned some of the most complex female characters. This piece would be right at home in a child's room or nursery. Teach them young that size doesn't determine power.

- ✖ ▸ 601
- ◗ ▸ 943
- N ▸ 745
- ς ▸ 761
- ✖ ▸ 3820

FITS A 5 × 7-INCH
(12.7 × 17.8 CM)
FRAME WHEN
STITCHED ON
14-COUNT AIDA

BEAUTY IS NOT A NUMBER

This important message emphasizes that there is no wrong way to have a body and that beauty is not in any way measured by the weight of that body. This can be a powerful reminder that you are beautiful regardless of your size.

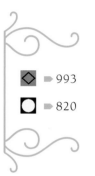

◆ ▬ 993

◖ ▬ 820

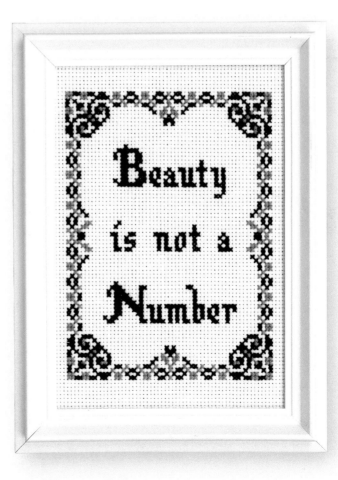

FITS A 5 × 7-INCH
(10.2 × 15.2 CM)
FRAME WHEN
STITCHED ON
14-COUNT AIDA

DAILY TO-DO LIST

Everyone's life is inevitably full of lists: action-item lists at work, grocery lists, lists of family activities, lists of gifts to buy, packing lists, lists of places to go. . . . This is a different kind of list, featuring reminders of things we should all do daily. Hang this piece in a place where you can see it every day, and resolve to take care of yourself and others.

□ ▸ 310

◪ ▸ 3857

⬆ ▸ 3848

♲ ▸ 3727

▶ ▸ 3348

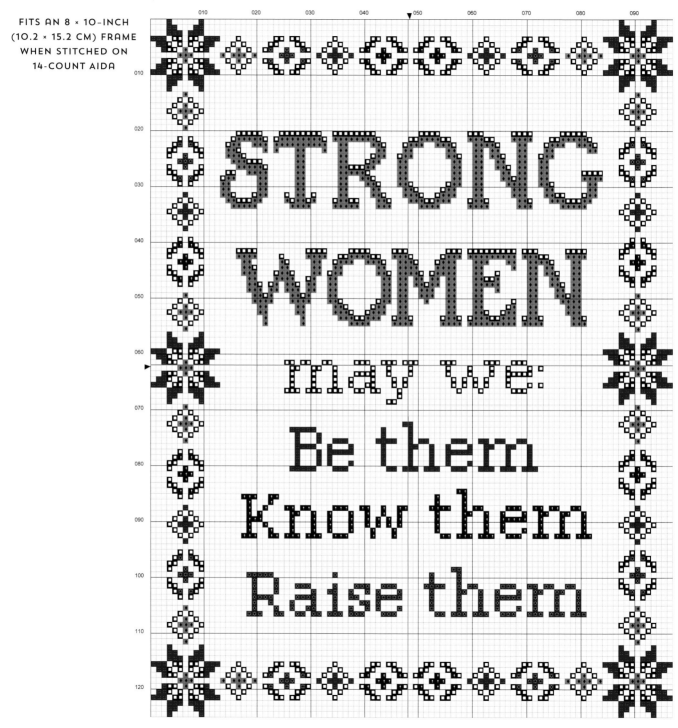

STRONG WOMEN

This large pattern proclaims in bold colors your goal to celebrate and embrace all the strong women in your life. The geometric border is inspired by traditional cross-stitch samplers and quilt-block designs.

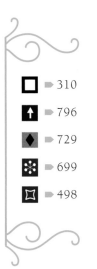

◻ ▸	310
⬆ ▸	796
◆ ▸	729
✳ ▸	699
◳ ▸	498

STAUNCH

Some people like to describe themselves as "strident" feminists, but I've always preferred "staunch." To me, the word means strong, steadfast, and loyal. This piece features a more complex Art Nouveau–inspired border.

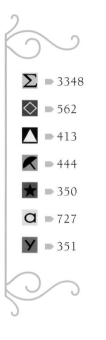

Σ	3348
◇	562
▲	413
◤	444
★	350
a	727
y	351

NOT YOUR BABE

Street harassment has probably existed since the invention of streets. While *babe* is one of the more innocuous words that someone could yell at you, comments like these are meant to make you feel small, helpless, and unwelcome in public spaces. This phrase proclaims that you are not any of those things and don't belong to anyone.

◨ ➠	563
n ➠	550
◖ ➠	729
▬ ➠	676

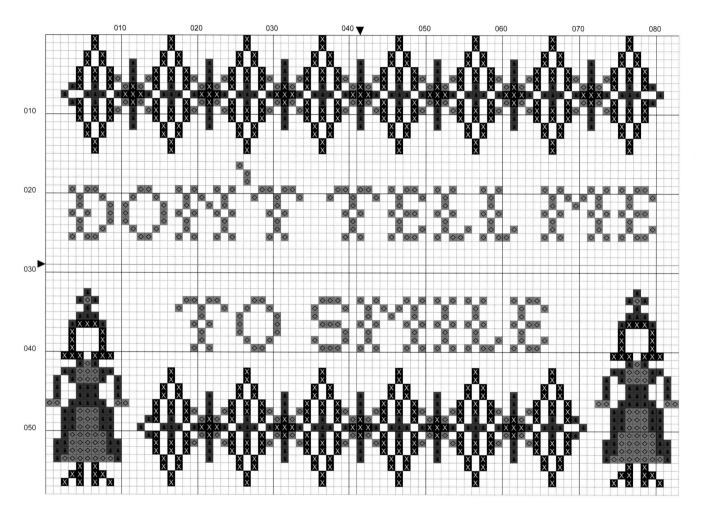

DON'T TELL ME TO SMILE

Many antique folk art designs feature figures of little ladies, usually doing some sort of housework. I incorporated two folk art ladies standing their ground instead, which is an especially appropriate response to being told to smile by male family members, coworkers, and even strangers on the street. The expectation for women to appear happy is a subtle form of sexism that demands them to look attractive and be agreeable for others despite how they actually feel. This piece makes it clear that you are not here to look good for others. *That's* something to smile about.

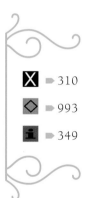

X	310
◇	993
⚑	349

CONSENT IS REQUIRED

Slogans like "Consent Is Sexy" mean well, but I don't think they go far enough when it comes to emphasizing the importance of consent. Consent is required, and everyone should make sure they understand that, continuously and enthusiastically. (Actually, that *is* pretty sexy. . . .)

☐ ▸	939
◆ ▸	817
◖ ▸	562
✚ ▸	156
C ▸	162
◓ ▸	818
☽ ▸	760

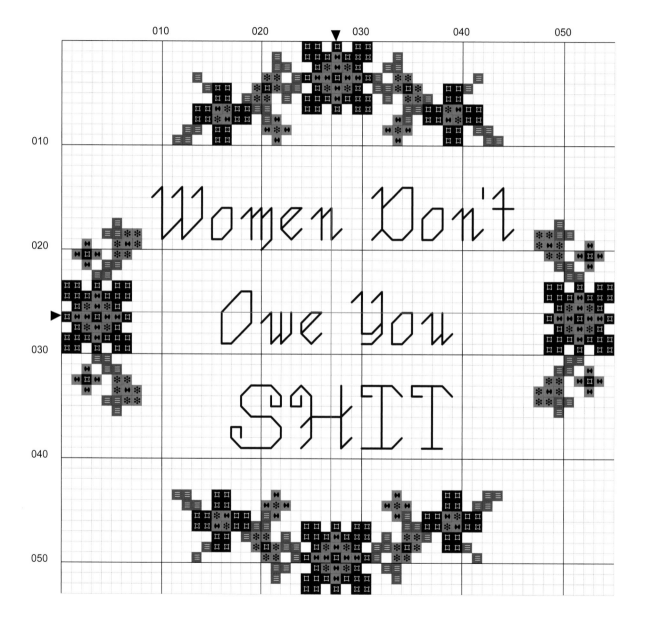

WOMEN DON'T OWE YOU SHIT

Feel free to show this sweet and snarky little hoop to anyone with an unjustified sense of entitlement to women's attention and energy. Whether it's your time, access to your body, or your emotional labor, you don't need to feel obligated to give anything to anyone. This design is a fun way to practice using the backstitch to add text on a small piece.

- ▣ ➤ 550
- ▤ ➤ 3812
- ▰ ➤ 3846
- ✳ ➤ 729

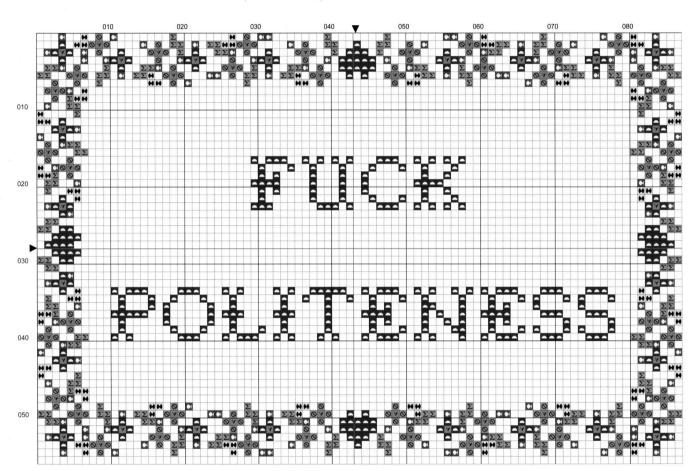

FUCK POLITENESS

This phrase, popularized by the podcast *My Favorite Murder*, references how the social pressure to avoid making a scene or being seen as inconsiderate can get women killed. The phrase "Fuck politeness" isn't about being rude on a regular basis; it's about finding the power to speak up when something doesn't seem right and to remove yourself from a potentially dangerous situation, even when it isn't "polite" to do so. This piece will remind you that it's not your job to make other people comfortable.

▶ 3848
▶ 210
▶ 917
▶ 164
▶ 352
▶ 445

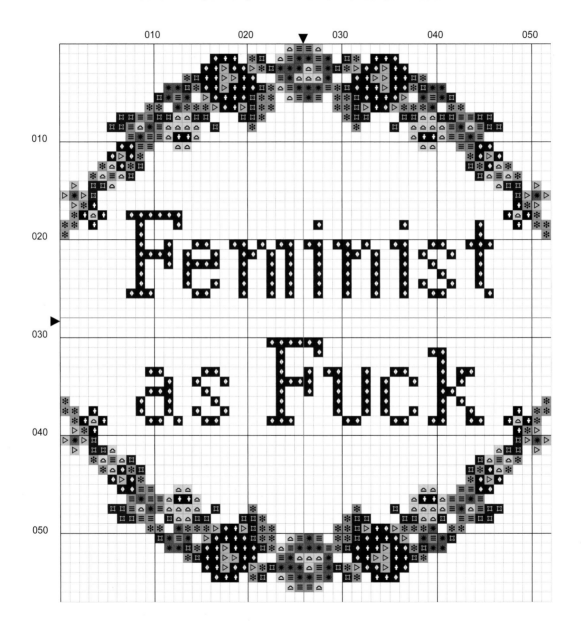

FEMINIST AS FUCK

Displaying this piece will make absolutely certain that everyone knows you not only identify as a feminist but are also proud to be one.

◈	▶	333
✳	▶	946
≡	▶	722
◠	▶	744
✳	▶	164
▣	▶	319
▷	▶	211
╂	▶	154

ASK ME ABOUT MY FEMINIST AGENDA

The "feminist agenda" means vastly different things to different people, but this pattern will help you proclaim that you do indeed have one and are happy to let people know what it entails. When presented with this cheerful and bright piece, someone will surely ask.

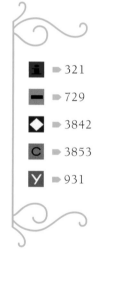

▪	➤ 321
▬	➤ 729
◇	➤ 3842
C	➤ 3853
Y	➤ 931

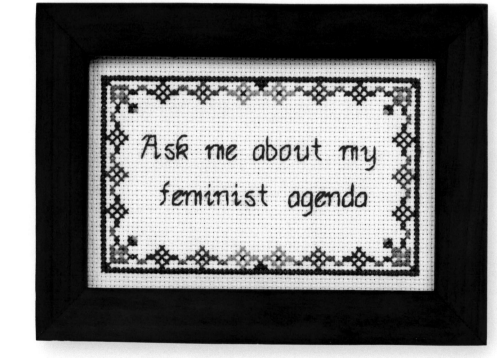

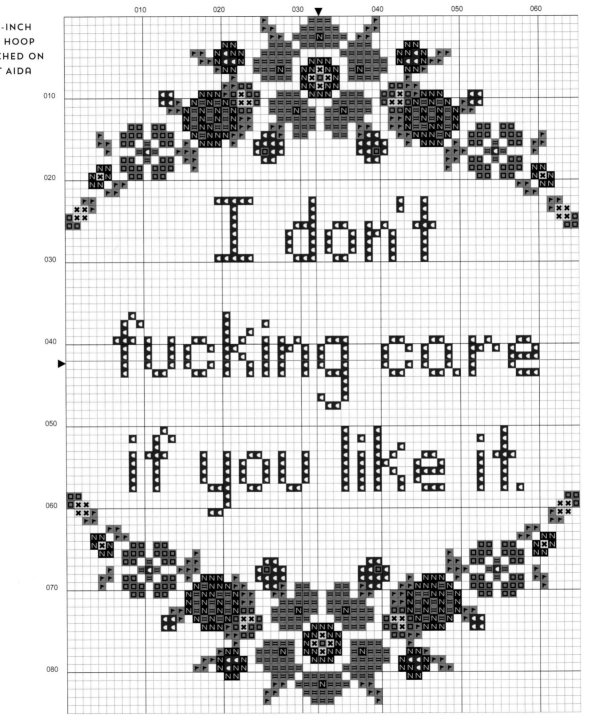

I DON'T FUCKING CARE IF YOU LIKE IT

This straightforward sentiment can be applied to almost anything: your art, your body, your choices, and your opinions. This piece uses particularly bold floss colors so that you can unashamedly display these blunt words. The intricate floral border makes it best for more practiced stitchers.

◖ ▸ 917
N ▸ 796
🔳 ▸ 3846
⬜ ▸ 352
▶ ▸ 471
✖ ▸ 445

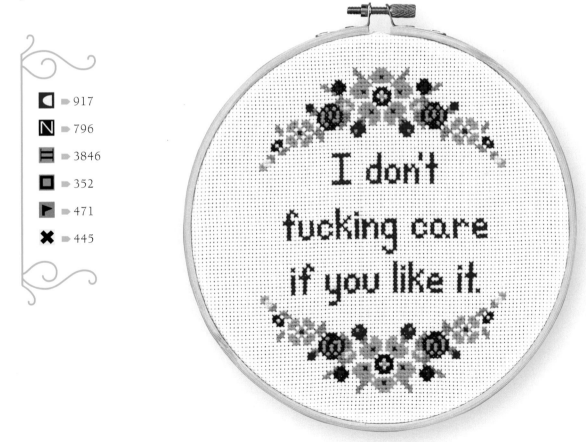

FUCK YOUR INTERNALIZED MISOGYNY

Internalized misogyny is sneaky. It rears its ugly head whenever a woman thinks or behaves toward other women or herself in a way that reinforces or relies on negative stereotypes about her gender. Hang this design as a reminder to fight against these beliefs, especially if you find yourself judging, mistrusting, or putting down yourself or others. This design includes strong little cross-stitched folk art ladies symbolizing women standing together, working together, and supporting one another.

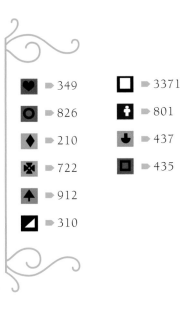

FITS AN 8 × 10-INCH
(20.3 × 25.4 CM)
FRAME WHEN
STITCHED ON
14-COUNT AIDA

Carry
yourself
with the
confidence
of a mediocre
white man.

CARRY YOURSELF WITH THE CONFIDENCE OF A MEDIOCRE WHITE MAN

Use this piece to remind yourself to hold your head high, as if you possess all the privilege of a straight, white, cisgender man. This pattern is one of the more challenging pieces in the book, especially if you're stitching on black Aida, which can be tricky. If using black Aida, remember to backlight your fabric to make the holes more visible.

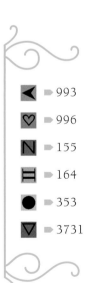

◄ ▶ 993

♡ ▶ 996

N ▶ 155

⊟ ▶ 164

● ▶ 353

▽ ▶ 3731

POLITICALLY ACTIVE

Feminism has always been inherently political. The patterns here are inspired by quotes from politicians and public figures, or by reactions to political events. I hope these designs will also inspire you to take action, whether by voting, contacting your representatives, or getting involved in campaigns, organizations, and causes that you are passionate about.

FITS A 4 × 6-INCH (10.2 × 15.2 CM) FRAME WHEN STITCHED ON 14-COUNT AIDA

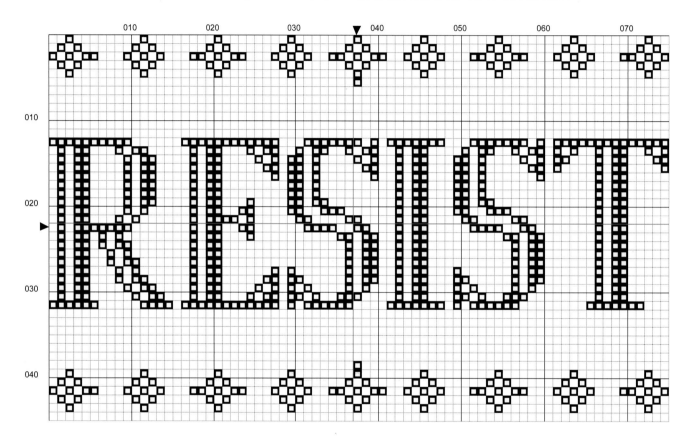

RESIST

Sometimes the best statement is a simple one. This call to action can mean whatever you want it to. How will you resist? With your vote? By participating in marches and protests? With your art? With self-care? No matter what you choose, this simple pattern makes an easy-to-stitch reminder to fight against injustice in whatever way you can. Use a colorful background fabric to make this simple monochromatic design pop.

☐ ▬ 310

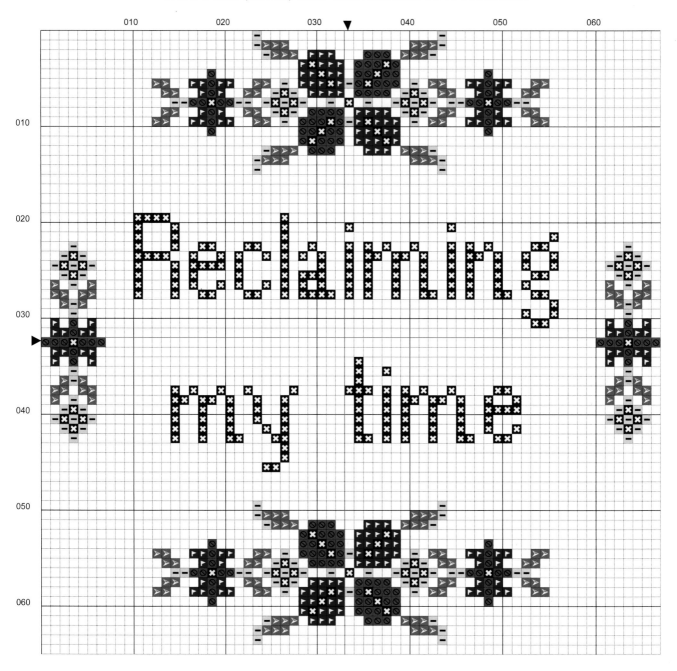

RECLAIMING MY TIME

"Reclaiming my time" became a rallying cry, a slogan, and even a meme after US Congress-woman Maxine Waters made use of it during a congressional hearing. She refused to let others dodge her questions or avoid accountability. This became a catchphrase that voiced the sentiments of any woman who has had her time wasted, been interrupted, or even been ignored by someone in an official or workplace setting.

☒	⬛	3799
⊳	⬛	992
⊘	⬛	334
▬	⬛	504
◥	⬛	552

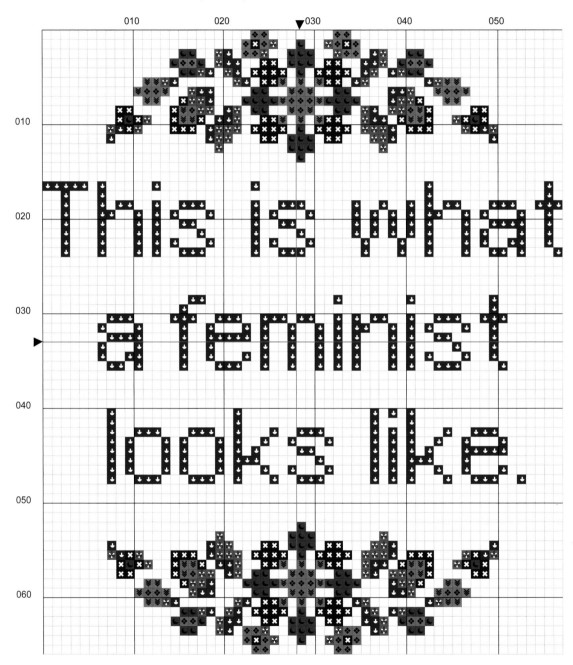

THIS IS WHAT A FEMINIST LOOKS LIKE

Anyone can identify as a feminist, and everyone should. Patriarchy harms not just women but men and nonbinary people as well. There is no wrong way to look like a feminist.

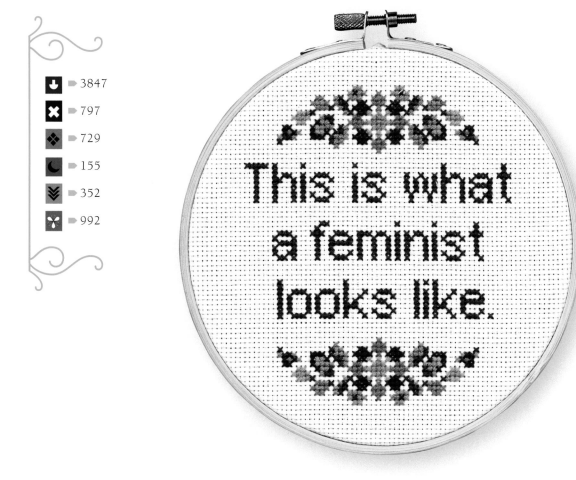

- ⬇ ▸ 3847
- ✖ ▸ 797
- ◆ ▸ 729
- ☾ ▸ 155
- ⏬ ▸ 352
- ⚜ ▸ 992

NASTY WOMAN & BAD HOMBRE

The day after Donald Trump spoke these words during a presidential debate with Hillary Rodham Clinton, I stitched up this set of patterns. Like other designs in this book, these two patterns are about reclaiming insulting words and turning them into a point of pride. They can be displayed on their own or as a pair.

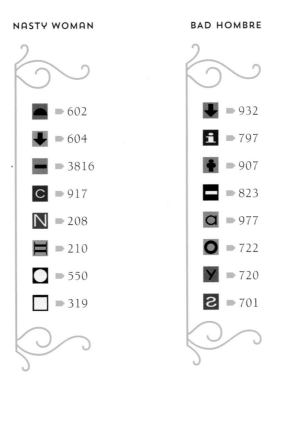

NASTY WOMAN		BAD HOMBRE	
⬤	▸ 602	⬇	▸ 932
⬇	▸ 604	🅸	▸ 797
▬	▸ 3816	✚	▸ 907
C	▸ 917	▬	▸ 823
N	▸ 208	α	▸ 977
⊟	▸ 210	O	▸ 722
O	▸ 550	Y	▸ 720
☐	▸ 319	Ƨ	▸ 701

WHEN THEY GO LOW, WE GO HIGH

Michelle Obama inspired us to take the high road with this famous quote from her speech at the 2016 Democratic National Convention. This piece is a great reminder to rise above the behavior of your opponent when the discourse gets ugly. This stitched piece with fun but simple florals can be hung in any office, classroom, or home.

- ◆ ▸ 413
- ℹ ▸ 210
- ✳ ▸ 913
- ▬ ▸ 743
- ⓐ ▸ 353
- ↗ ▸ 164
- ⧈ ▸ 519

FITS A 6 × 8-INCH
(10.2 × 15.2 CM)
FRAME WHEN
STITCHED ON
16-COUNT AIDA

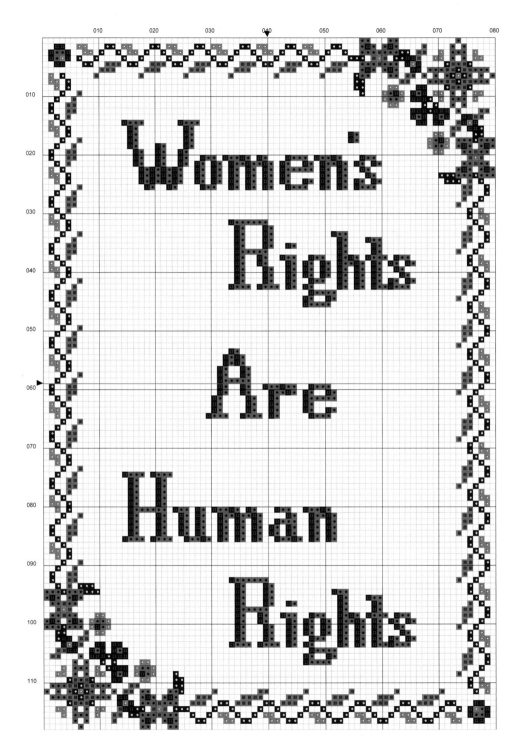

WOMEN'S RIGHTS ARE HUMAN RIGHTS

The idea that women's rights and human rights are one and the same was first put in writing in the 1830s by female abolitionists. The concept has since been used by many feminist leaders, but perhaps one of the best-known uses of this particular phrase came during Hillary Rodham Clinton's speech at the United Nations Fourth World Conference on Women in 1995. This quote is still relevant today, especially when many rights, such as access to education, reproductive rights, and freedom from gender-related violence, are considered up for debate. It seems like a lot of people could still use this reminder.

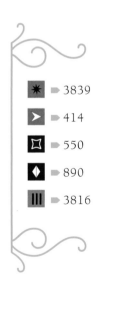

✳ ▸	3839
▶ ▸	414
▣ ▸	550
◆ ▸	890
▥ ▸	3816

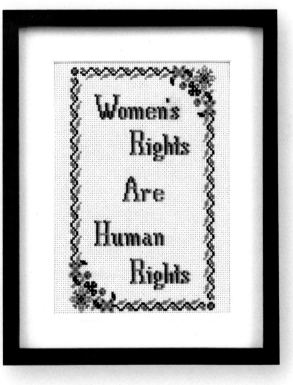

NEVERTHELESS, SHE PERSISTED

US Senator Mitch McConnell attempted to silence fellow senator Elizabeth Warren during a confirmation hearing with these words. But rather than affirm the idea that women should stay quiet and keep their opinions to themselves, the words became a call for women never to give up and to stand up for what they believe. The geometric border on this design includes many hidden Venus symbols mixed together to make a strong structure around the words. I used pink to create the ombré effect, but it would work with any four colors going from dark to light.

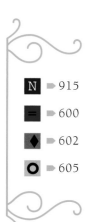

N	▶ 915
=	▶ 600
◆	▶ 602
O	▶ 605

She was warned.
She was given
an explanation.
Nevertheless,
she persisted.

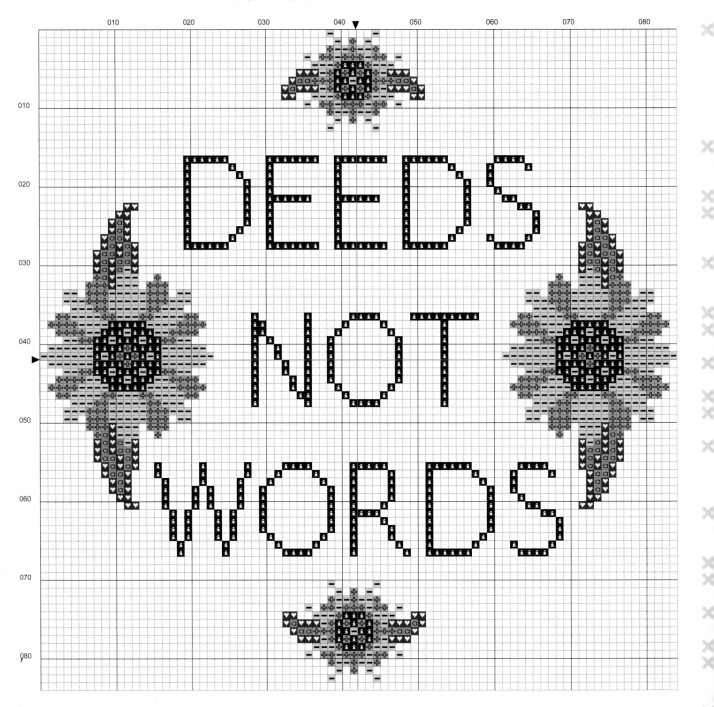

DEEDS NOT WORDS

This piece is a love letter to the women's suffrage movement and an ode to the women who fought for the right to vote on both sides of the pond. In the United States, the sunflower was a popular symbol of the cause. Elizabeth Cady Stanton and Susan B. Anthony adopted the Kansas state flower as a symbol of the suffrage movement when Kansas was considering passing a women's voting referendum. "Deeds not Words" was coined by British suffragette Emmeline Pankhurst and became a motto of the UK suffrage movement.

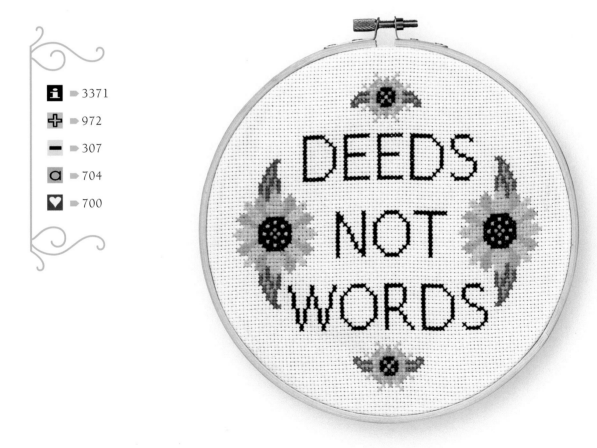

ⓘ	3371
✚	972
▬	307
ⓐ	704
♥	700

A WOMAN'S PLACE IS IN THE REVOLUTION

This take on the traditional (and outdated) saying "a woman's place is in the home" was one of the first feminist cross-stitch designs I created. I carried a blown-up version of this piece on a poster at the Women's March in Chicago in January 2017. I see it as a message to keep working for equality, regardless of where that work may take you.

Symbol	Color	Symbol	Color
▼	▶ 604	⚡	▶ 676
◘	▶ 924	◖	▶ 550
♣	▶ 742	☰	▶ 3835
♥	▶ 818	✳	▶ 211
✖	▶ 349		
◤	▶ 164		
◉	▶ 986		
▷	▶ 3755		

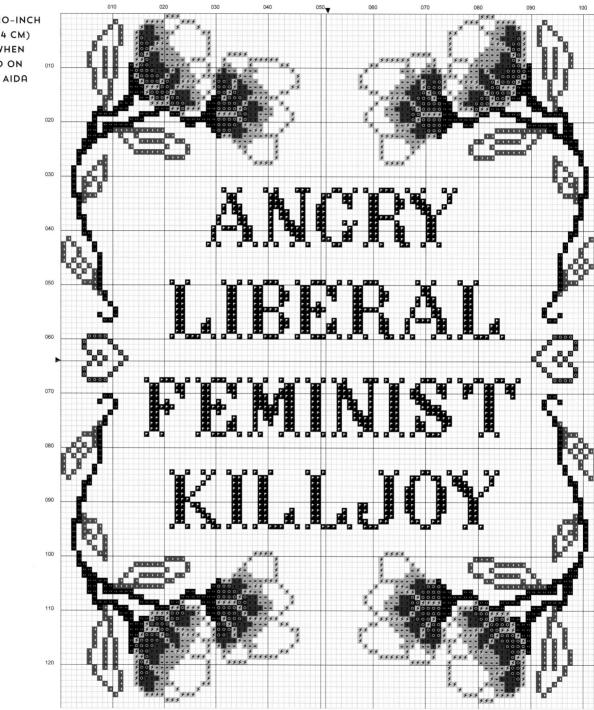

ANGRY LIBERAL FEMINIST KILLJOY

Just because you habitually call out people's problematic statements and shut down sexist jokes doesn't mean you don't like fun; it just means you don't like sexism. This piece is a great way to turn negative words into something positive. Embrace what you are. You don't need to apologize for not being "fun," especially when there are plenty of other things to be angry about. This ornate piece is a large project that will let you display your identity like the badge of honor it is.

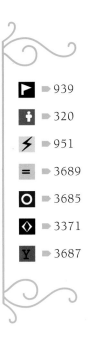

▶ ➡ 939

🇫 ➡ 320

⚡ ➡ 951

= ➡ 3689

◉ ➡ 3685

◈ ➡ 3371

Y ➡ 3687

LGBTQ PRIDE FLAG

The feminist movement could not be complete without acknowledging and embracing the LGBTQIA community, which has been fighting to accomplish many of the same equality-focused goals. Display this modern and easy-to-stitch take on the iconic pride flag when you want to let people know they are safe and welcome. If you would rather stitch the traditional pride flag, simply fill in the outlined rectangles with stitches of the same color.

349
721
725
702
820
550

FITS A 2 × 3-INCH (5.1 × 7.6 CM) FRAME WHEN STITCHED ON 14-COUNT AIDA

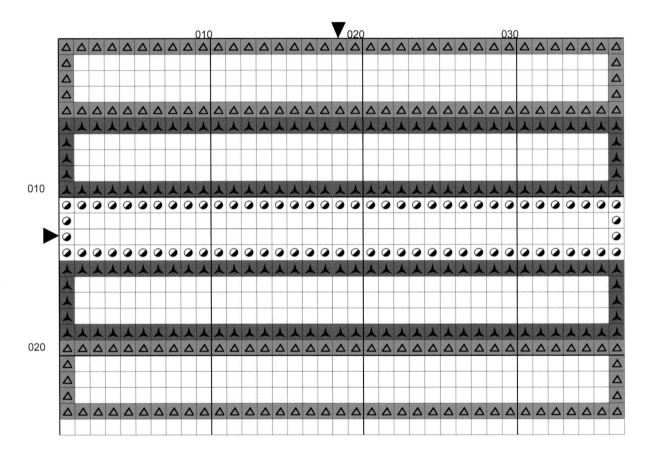

TRANSGENDER PRIDE FLAG

Feminism is not just for cisgender women. The inclusion and visibility of trans, gender-fluid, and nonbinary individuals is key to intersectional feminism. As with the pride flag, display this piece as a symbol of your own identity or as a message that all are welcome and accepted. Stitching it on black fabric will make it stand out even more. If you would rather stitch the traditional transgender pride flag, simply fill in the outlined rectangles with stitches of the same color.

◐ ▶ 5200

▲ ▶ 603

△ ▶ 519

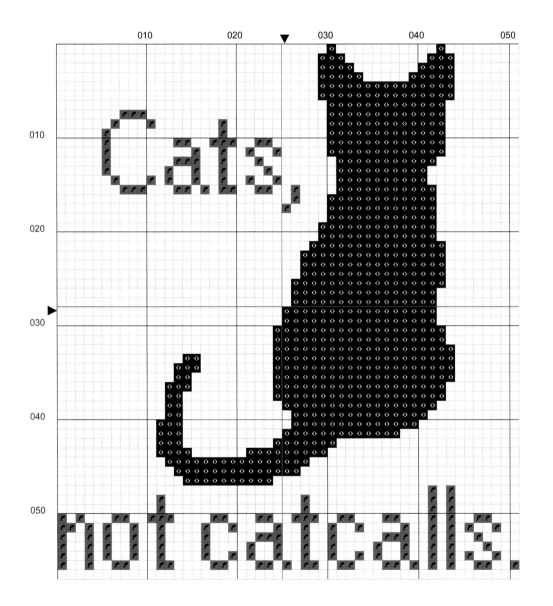

CATS, NOT CATCALLS

This wouldn't truly be a cross-stitch book without a cat-themed pattern. Cats have been a traditional motif in cross-stitch for decades. This small and simple design turns the often misogynistic "cat lady" stereotype on its head and also takes a stand against street harassment. (Not to mention the little kitty is just so cute.)

◆ ▶ 310

🐾 ▶ 3851

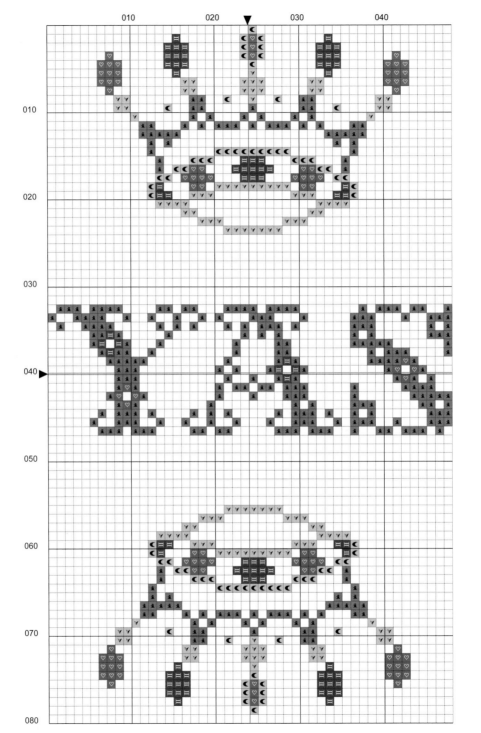

"YAS QUEEN" CROWNS

If you want to try a piece on black Aida, this would be the one to start with. "Yas" and "yas queen" are encouraging exclamations that originated in the queer community and can be traced to the 1980s drag ball scene in New York. Like many phrases from that community, "yas queen" has now entered the mainstream. In addition to shouting the phrase as a show of support, you can now stitch and display it always. The crowns in this design are here to honor all feminist queens.

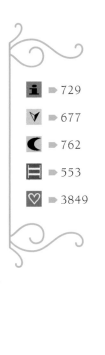

- ➧ 729
- ➧ 677
- ➧ 762
- ➧ 553
- ➧ 3849

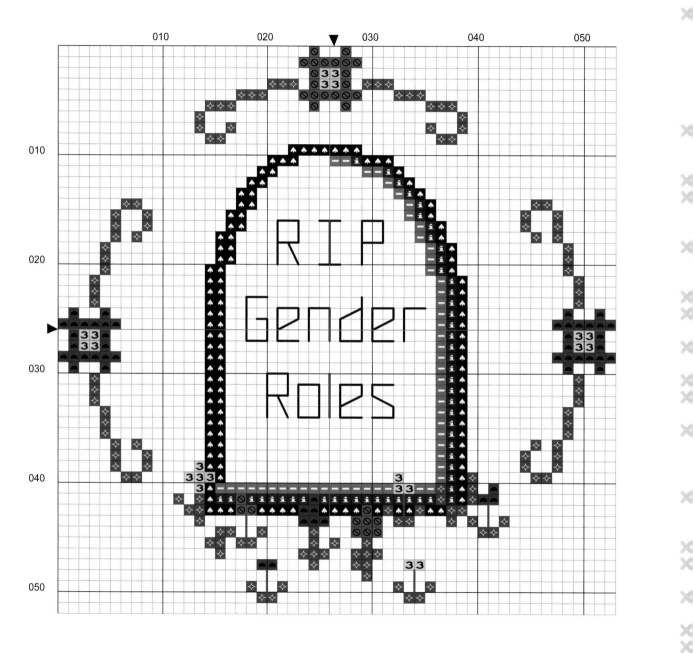

RIP GENDER ROLES

This morbidly cheeky little piece memorializes the death of all traditional gender roles, not just those for women. Patriarchy is toxic for everyone. Insisting that boys can't be sensitive or emotional is just as limiting as insisting that girls can't be strong, loud, or dominant. Insisting that gender must only be binary can be equally harmful. Hopefully, stitching this design will give you the courage to lay these damaging stereotypes to rest for good. This piece uses backstitch to create the letters and details of the image.

- ➡ 3799
- ➡ 3855
- ➡ 340
- ➡ 3687
- ➡ 988
- ➡ 317
- ➡ 318

MALE TEARS

This pattern is a wicked take on a classic image of girlhood and femininity: the tea party! The design is best for intermediate stitchers due to its many colors and asymmetrical florals.

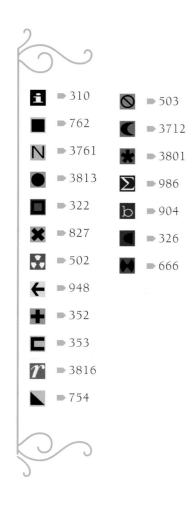

ℹ	▶ 310	⊘	▶ 503	
■	▶ 762	◖	▶ 3712	
N	▶ 3761	✳	▶ 3801	
●	▶ 3813	Σ	▶ 986	
◼	▶ 322	b	▶ 904	
✖	▶ 827	◀	▶ 326	
☢	▶ 502	⋈	▶ 666	
←	▶ 948			
✚	▶ 352			
⊏	▶ 353			
r	▶ 3816			
◣	▶ 754			

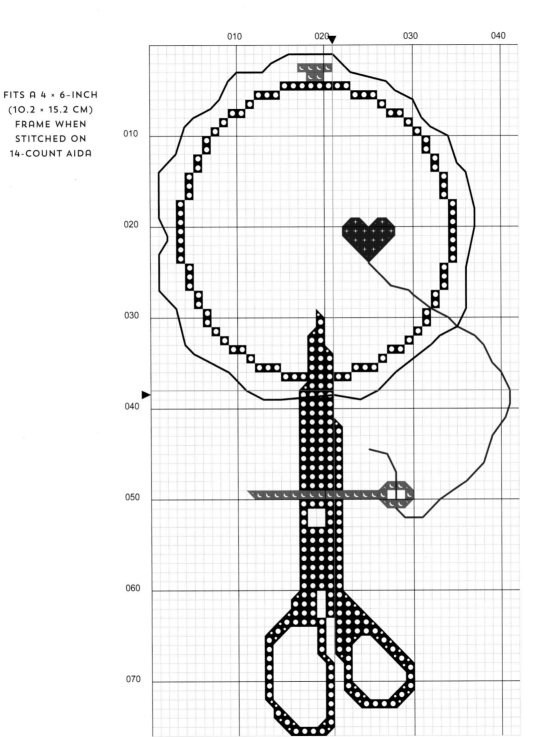

FITS A 4 × 6-INCH
(10.2 × 15.2 CM)
FRAME WHEN
STITCHED ON
14-COUNT AIDA

TOOLS OF RESISTANCE

In this piece, I fashioned my chosen tools of resistance into the Venus symbol. It is an ode to the items I use in my craftivism. I stitched the design on Fiddler's Cloth Aida; the oatmeal color and variegated details give the piece a more rustic look. This project is best for an intermediate stitcher, as it includes a fair amount of backstitch detail.

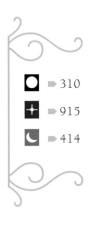

- ⬤ ▶ 310
- ✛ ▶ 915
- 🌙 ▶ 414

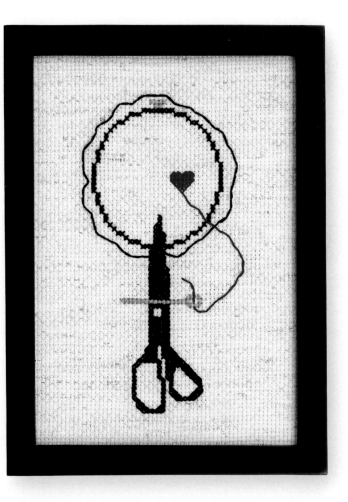

ROSIE THE RIVETER

This iconic image of Rosie the Riveter appeared on the "We Can Do It!" poster and encouraged women to work jobs traditionally reserved for men during World War II. The painting on the poster was inspired by a news photo of Naomi Parker Fraley, taken while she was assembling aircrafts at Naval Air Station Alameda. Today Rosie the Riveter remains an emblem of the strength, economic empowerment, and financial independence that comes with being a working woman—something that was more novel in the early 1940s. The vintage look of this design pairs perfectly with the art of cross-stitch. This pattern is split over four pages. The gray areas show four-row sections that repeat parts of the pattern appearing on previous pages. These repeated sections make it easier to see one part of the design in relation to another. It is the most challenging pattern in the book and best for a more experienced stitcher or someone looking for a long-term project. Don't worry, you can do it!

3865	758	517	826	156	3774
951	402	825	939	797	3078
967	3778	3858	225	798	712
818	819	803	356	632	3747
754	3770	221	3859	799	158
3824	948	823	746	801	3328
945	3776	336	761	3772	349
353	3856	820	347	938	
3771	3779	824	152	760	

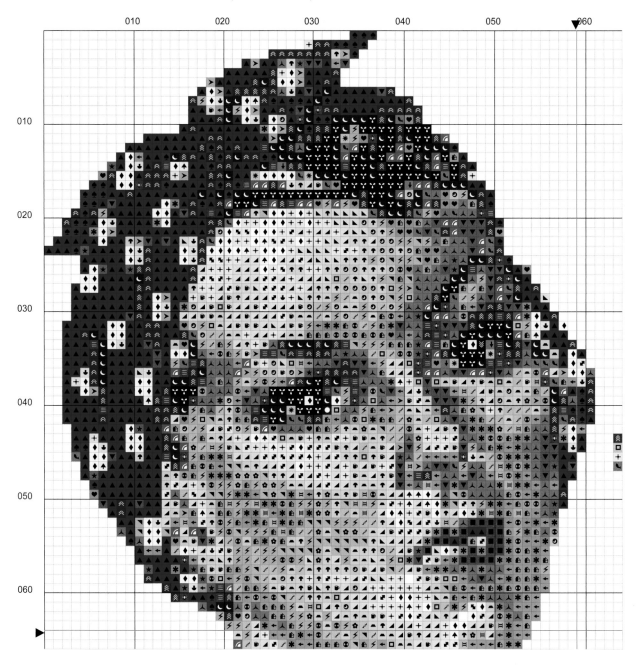

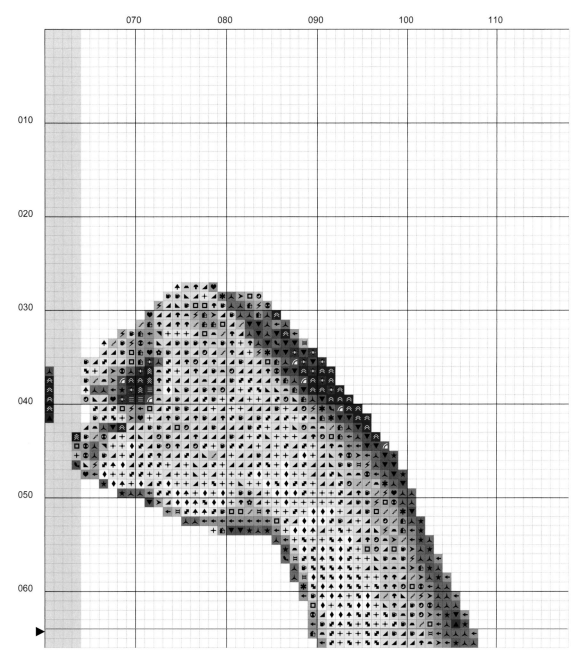

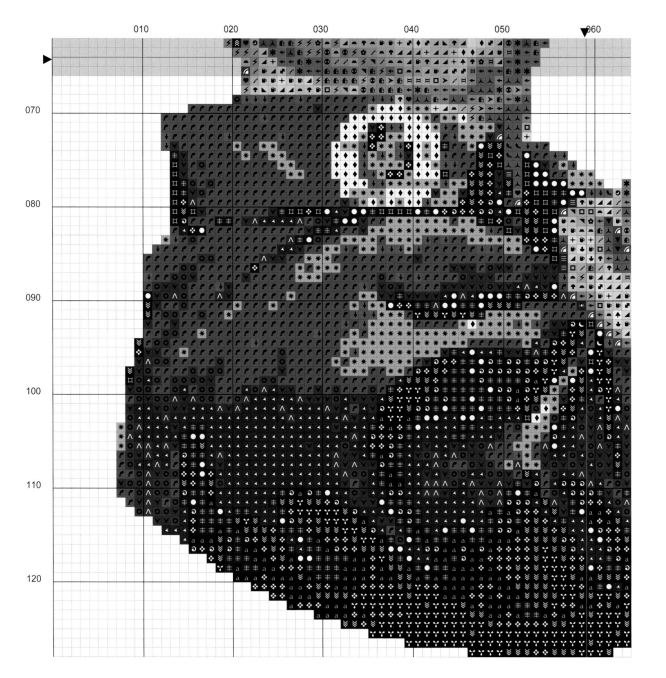

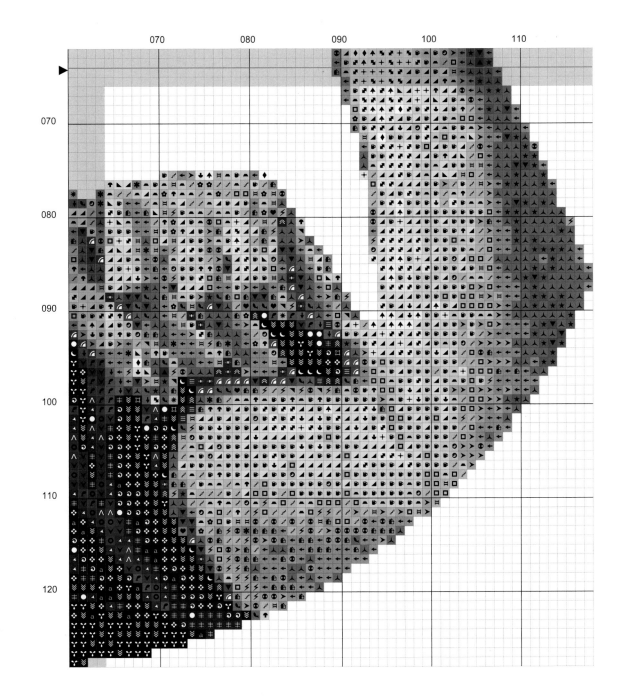

RESOURCES

"Where can I buy all of these cross-stitch supplies?" you ask. Here are some answers!

PATTERNS AND KITS

Are you in search of more to stitch? You can find digital patterns from small handmade businesses and independent designers, as well as DIY kits that include all of the supplies you need for a project.

ETSY

etsy.com

There are hundreds of cross-stitch designers on this online marketplace offering instant download patterns as well as full cross-stitch kits. You can search the entire site for patterns that appeal to you or find a designer you love and shop at their individual store.

SUBVERSIVE CROSS STITCH

subversivecrossstitch.com

An originator of the modern cross-stitch movement, this site sells patterns, kits, and supplies.

BADASS CROSS STITCH

badasscrossstitch.com

This site offers both cross-stitch and embroidery patterns, most with a craftivist bent and many of them for free.

THE HOOP AND NEEDLE

thehoopandneedle.com

This excellent independent shop stocks kits from various cross-stitch and embroidery designers.

SUPPLIES

I highly recommend finding and supporting local needlework and craft shops in your area. A quick online search should show you nearby options. Savvy thrifters have been known to find treasure troves of cheap cross-stitch supplies at secondhand stores. If these are not available in your area, there are also a few great chain stores and online resources you could check out.

JOANN FABRICS

joann.com

MICHAELS

michaels.com

If you're in the US, both JoAnn Fabrics and Michaels are great chain store options for finding craft supplies. They each have an online shop as well.

DMC

DMC.com

DMC is one of the largest producers of embroidery floss. You will find their floss in most US stores, but you can also buy floss from them directly, as well as with hoops and other supplies.

123STITCH

123stitch.com

This very comprehensive online option carries lots of supplies from different brands. It could be an especially good resource if there are few brick-and-mortar craft shops in your area.

EVERYTHING CROSS STITCH

everythingcrossstitch.com

The name says it all. This site has a plethora of supplies as well as full kits.

ACKNOWLEDGMENTS

Thank you to anyone who stitches my patterns for trusting me with your hobby, your therapy, your art.

Eternal gratitude to my coven of stitchers: Courtney Abbott, Brianna Borger, John Cockerill, Caitlin DeLong, Claire Keating, Laura Keating, Whitney Morse, Makha Mthembu, Kelley Ristow, and Ann Rohr. I could not have done it without you.

Big thanks to my subversively stitchy mentor, Julie Jackson, for her kind ears and straight talk; my agent Lori Galvin and everyone at Aevitas Creative Management; my editor Elysia Liang and the Sterling Publishing team: Kayla Overbey, Hannah Reich, Shannon Nicole Plunkett, Lorie Pagnozzi, Elizabeth Mihaltse Lindy, and Chris Bain; Marianne Philbin, Lesley Ware, and Nicole Taylor, who taught me "how to book"; Jenna Schoppe and Kate Adams for encouragement since the very beginning (sorry for all the needles in the couch); Michelle Kritselis, Anna Schutz, Melissa Bellows, Jonas Davidow, William Panek, Nick Shoda, Justin Harner, Sophie Alderson, Annabel Keith, and Deanna Drake for being early cheerleaders and supporters; and the artist and maker communities of Chicago and Midwest Craft Con.

Extra-special thanks to T. J. Anderson, who takes care of me when I forget to. You are my dear.

Love and thanks to my wonderfully supportive family: my parents Ann and Matt Rohr; brother Danny and sister Theresa; Grandma Dee and Grandpa Tom; aunts Denise, Janet, Katharine, Lisa, Margaret, Martha, and Sarah; uncles Alex, Ray, and Tom; cousins Anna, Brad, Casey, Claire, Emma, and Laura.

Love and thanks to the family with me in memory: Ann C. Rohr, Richard Rohr, Michael Wood, and especially Tio Tom. I strive to make art and teach art as well as you did.

ABOUT THE AUTHOR

STEPHANIE ROHR grew up in Naperville, Illinois, and lives in Chicago. After stitching for fun most of her life, she started her cross-stitch business, stephXstitch, in 2010. In addition to being a cross-stitch artist and designer, Stephanie is an actor, director, singer, and voice teacher. Stephanie holds a BFA from Drake University and an MA from University of the Arts, London. When not cross-stitching, performing, or teaching, she enjoys true-crime podcasts, questionable television, playing piano, riding her bike, and petting other people's dogs. You can find hundreds more patterns, kits, pieces, and information about in-person events and classes at stephXstitch.com. She is also on Etsy, Facebook, and Instagram (@stephXstitch).

INDEX

Note: Page numbers in *italics* indicate patterns.

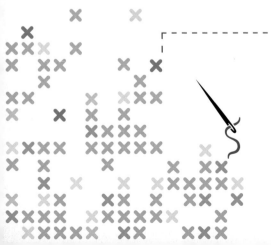